# Danny learns The Fourth Commandment

Written and Illustrated
by Christabel N Pankhurst

Dedicated to
parents and children everywhere,
who seek the love of God

WHERE UNTO A LITTLE CHILD
IN JESUS NAME IS GIVEN,
REMEMBERED BY OUR LORD
SHALL BE,
WHEN WE HAVE ENTERED HEAVEN

AND YET AGAIN IN HOLY WRIT;
THESE GRACIOUS WORDS WE SEE
"HE WHO RECEIVES A LITTLE CHILD,
HE THEN RECEIVETH ME."

L.S.

For Daniel O'Loughlin
Children's Picture Book
Published by Queen of Angels Publishing.
Cappanabogha, Leap, Skibbereen. County Cork.
Ireland


Danny Learns The Fourth Commandment
Paperback Edition

EAN  0956009654
ISBN  9780956009654

Text Copyright 2010 Christabel N Pankhurst
Illustrations Copyright 2010 Christabel N Pankhurst

Cover design by Finian Pankhurst
Queen of Angels Publishing.


website: www.queenofangelspublishing.org

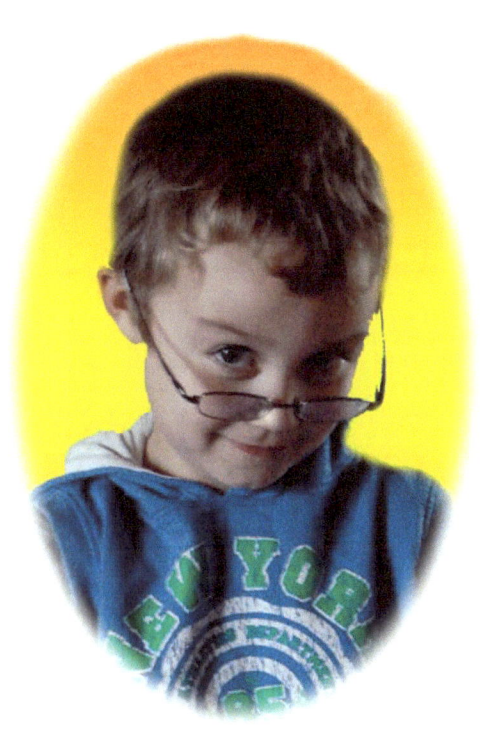

Danny felt very pleased with himself.

He was learning the Ten Commandments.

Danny had learned the first three commandments off by heart.

Last night he was able to say the Fourth Commandment, without making any mistakes. Standing at his mother's knee, Danny slowly and carefully said,

**"Fourth Commandment honour thy father and thy mother."**
Papa asked,
   "What does it mean Danny?"
Danny knew the answer to that.
     "It means that I must do what my parents tell me."

"That's right Danny," Mama said, "You must be obedient."
"God gave us His Commandments for our protection." Mama explained, "When we tell you what to do, it is to keep you from harm because we love you."

"Oh" said Danny, "I will always do what you tell me!"

"We will see!" laughed Papa, "We will see!"

At Mass on Sunday Father Paul taught his congregation about the Ten Commandments.

When he talked about the Fourth Commandment, Father Paul told the children that Jesus was always obedient.

Father said, "Jesus is God, but He did what Our Lady and Saint Joseph told Him to do.

If you love Jesus you will keep His Commandments, you will do what ever your parents tell you."

Then Father gave out the announcements.

"I want a good strong boy to sweep around the Church Yard every Saturday morning." he said, "If you are interested in the job come to see me after Mass today."

'That's my job! That's my job!' sang Danny, in his head.

Now he found it hard to keep still.

Danny decided that when the consecration bell rang he would bow his head very low and practice piety.

Then he would ask Jesus to make sure Father Paul gave him the job.

When Mass was over Danny would run to Father Paul and ask for the job.

## Would Danny get the job?

## Yes! Danny got the job!

Father Paul said,
"Brush all around the Church. But do not leave the Churchyard.

Papa said, "Brush all around the Church.

But remember Danny, do not leave the Churchyard."

Danny worked hard all morning.

He wanted to do

his very best.

Danny used

the big brush.

He used the

wheelbarrow.

Danny swept the church porch.

Danny swept on both sides of the Church.

Danny was very careful not to leave the Church yard.

He would just finish brushing the pathway as far as the new graveyard. Suddenly he heard a loud meeeow!

It was Fluffy the Churchyard Cat.

"Oh Fluffy!" exclaimed Danny.

This was the first time Danny had ever been so close to Fluffy.

'Fluffy must like me best,' Danny thought proudly to himself. 'All my friends will envy me when they see me playing with Fluffy.'

Suddenly Fluffy shot off into the Church porch.

What was Fluffy looking at?

Danny called and called to Fluffy.

But Fluffy was not listening.

He was staring out across the graveyard.

Something was moving between the grave stones.

It was a rabbit!!

The rabbit was watching Fluffy.

Suddenly the rabbit scampered off.

He hid among the grave stones.

Fluffy crept silently through the old graveyard.

Fluffy was getting closer and closer to the rabbit.

Silently Fluffy crept out of the Church yard.

Then Fluffy dashed after the rabbit.

The rabbit raced across the field towards the meadow.

Soon the rabbit, followed by Fluffy, disappeared through the meadow gate.

Fluffy and the rabbit were nowhere to be seen.

"Come Back!" called Danny.

"Come Back Fluffy!"

Danny watched as Fluffy disappeared into the distance.

He knew the two runaways were headed to the meadow.

'I'll just run to the meadow gate,' thought Danny, 'I won't go any further than that.'

Danny ran all the way to the meadow gate.

He climbed up on the gate. He leaned over trying to see where Fluffy had gone.

"Fluffy!" Danny called.
The cat was nowhere to be seen.
"I will just run down the meadow and find Fluffy," Danny decided. "I will be back so quick no one will know I have left the Church yard."

Quickly Danny jumped down. He unfastened the gate.

He had to be quick or he would lose sight of Fluffy.
Danny saw that the sun had gone down in the West. It was getting darker so he would have to hurry.

As Danny ran he felt very proud of himself.

Fluffy wanted to be his friend.

Danny ran faster and faster.

Danny felt even more proud.

If he could run this fast he would surely win all the races at next school sports day.

Then something awful happened!

Danny tripped and he went tumbling over and over on the grass.

Danny tried to get to his feet.
OOOOuch! He cried out, as a pain shot through his knee.

Danny tried to walk.

"OOOOuch!" he cried again.

"Now my other knee is sore as well."

"How will I walk home" Danny wailed.

Danny sat back down again.

He looked closely at each ankle.

They didn't look swollen. But oh, his right ankle did hurt a lot.

Danny began to feel afraid.
He wished he had never left the Church yard.

Papa would be cross with him.
Mama would be cross with him.

How would anyone ever find him here in the meadow?

Danny said a little prayer to Jesus,

"Please dearest Jesus, send my Papa to find me and bring me home safely."

Papa came to look for Danny.
Papa looked all around the church yard.

"Daneeeee!" called Papa.
"Where are you?"

Papa looked all around the new graveyard.
"Daneeeeee!" he called again and again.

Papa walked through the old graveyard.
"Daneee!" Papa was very very worried.

Where oh where, had Danny gone?

Danny thought he could hear Papa calling in the distance. He decided to pray some more.

"Oh please, Our Lady and Saint Joseph" Danny prayed, "help my Papa find me, like you found Jesus in the temple."

Then Danny realised. He had left the temple. He had been told to stay around the Church yard and he had disobeyed. It was time to say an Act of Contrition. "Dear Jesus." Danny said sadly, "I am so sorry I offended you by disobeying my Mama and Papa. I have broken your Fourth Commandment. I will try very hard never to sin again."

"Papa! Papa!" Danny shouted as his father appeared at the gate to the meadow.

"What on earth are you doing Danny?" asked Papa.
"Why did you not come when I called? And why did you leave the Church yard?
How could you be so disobedient Danny?"

"Oh Papa, I'm so sorry I ran after Fluffy and he was running after a rabbit. Then I tumbled over and hurt my knees and my ankle. I can't walk home."

"We will have to think of some way to get you home." said Papa.

"Clever Papa!" exclaimed Danny. "I get to ride home in the wheel barrow."

Then Danny prayed, quietly to himself, "Thank you Jesus for helping Papa find me so quickly."

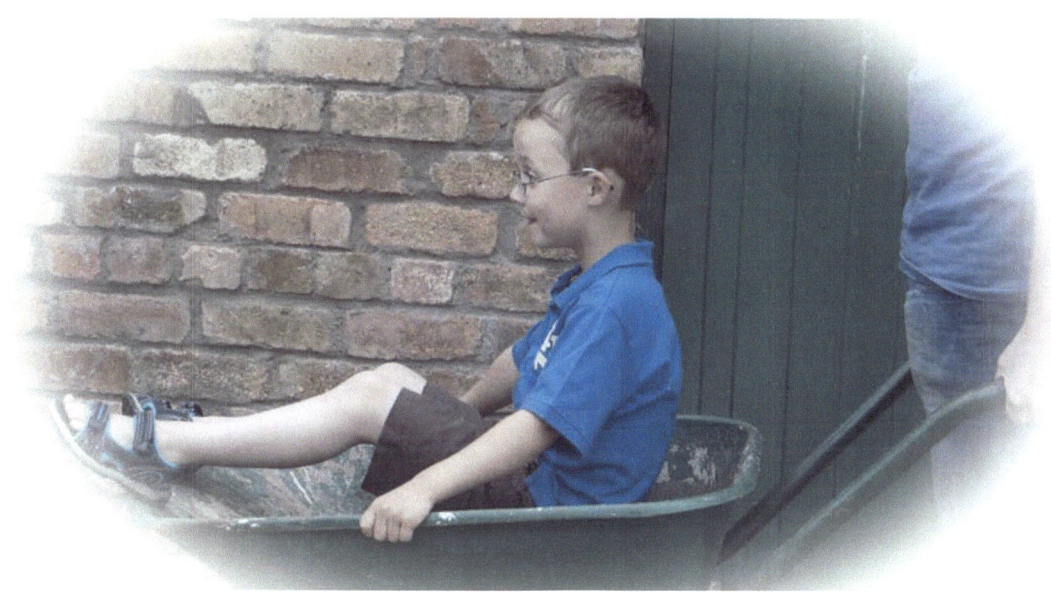

"I hope you have learned your lesson Danny."

Papa was still cross but he was so glad that Danny was safe.

By next Saturday Danny's legs were completely better. However Danny's wounded pride would take longer to heal. He had lost his job sweeping the Church yard, now instead he had to sweep and tidy the yard at home. Not half as much fun and no Fluffy to talk to.

"Danny!" Mama called from the kitchen, "Come inside. A letter has arrived for you."

It was a letter from Father Paul.

Dear Danny,

I am sorry to hear that you fell and hurt yourself in the meadow. You did a very good job of sweeping the Church yard on Saturday.

I have spoken to your Papa and we have agreed that an older boy will sweep the Church yard. However in a few years time you will be tall enough to learn to ring the Steeple Bell at the Consecration. You will be announcing to the world that Jesus is coming onto the altar.

Looking forward to seeing you at Mass on Sunday.

Fr. Paul

**Jesus loves all the children of the world.**

The next time Danny went to visit his Nanna, she read to him from the Bible. She read the story of 'The Finding of Jesus in The Temple.'

"You see Danny," Nanna said, "Jesus stopped doing what He wanted to do and instead, he did what Our Lady and Saint Joseph asked Him to do.

Jesus was obedient to them."

Nanna hugged Danny, "Jesus loves children very much and He wants you to know that if everyone in the whole world, kept all the Commandments, all the time; the world would be a wonderful place in which to live."

"Oh, don't you worry, Nanna," Danny assured her, "I won't be breaking the Fourth Commandment again."

"We will see!" smiled Nanna, "We will see!"

www.ingramcontent.com/pod-product-compliance
Lightning Source LLC
Chambersburg PA
CBHW041229040426
42444CB00002B/105